Decorative Painting
for the home

Decorative
Painting
for the home

Pat Osborne

New Holland

DEDICATION

This book is dedicated to my late parents, Betty and Tom, who were always there for me, and to my partner Mark for his unconditional support.

Acknowledgments

Special thanks go to Carol Sykes, DecoArt's UK Helping Artist Coordinator, for introducing me to decorative painting and to Stephanie Weightman of NCW Ltd/Plaid for her encouragement. They have both contributed projects to this book. I would also like to thank the other contributing artists: Ann Myers, Cynthia Horsfield, Paula Haley, Cathryn Wood and Beth Blinston.

Grateful thanks go to DecoArt, Plaid, NCW Ltd, Vale Woodcraft, Stencil House, Scumble Goosie, Walnut Hollow, Ikea, Raphael and Harvey Baker for providing products and props for photography. For more information see page 95.

Last, but not least, many thanks to the following artists who agreed to let their work feature in the Gallery pages of this book: Priscilla Hauser, one of my favourite artists, and Liz Bramhall.

CONTACT DETAILS FOR CONTRIBUTING ARTISTS:

Beth Blinston: www.blinston.homestead.com

Liz Bramhall: Tel: 0114 288 4299

Paula Haley: Tel: 01484 423 641

Priscilla Hauser: www.priscillahauser.com

Cynthia Horsfield: cynthia_horsfield@lineone.net

Ann Myers: Tel: 01609 777 787

Pat Osborne: pat@ukart.com; www.patosborne.co.uk

Carol Sykes: carolsykes@yahoo.co.uk; www.carolsykes.co.uk

Stephanie Weightman: sales@ncw.co.uk; www.ukonestroke.com

Cathryn Wood: www.cathryns.co.uk

Published in 2003 by
New Holland Publishers (UK) Ltd
London · Cape Town · Sydney · Auckland

Garfield House, 86–88 Edgware Road
London W2 2EA
United Kingdom
www.newhollandpublishers.com

80 McKenzie Street
Cape Town 8001
South Africa

Level 1, Unit 4, 14 Aquatic Drive
Frenchs Forest, NSW 2086
Australia

218 Lake Road
Northcote, Auckland
New Zealand

ISBN 1 84330 481 3

Senior Editor: Clare Sayer
Photographer: Shona Wood
Editorial Direction: Rosemary Wilkinson

10 9 8 7 6 5 4 3 2 1

Reproduction by
Pica Digital Pte., Singapore
Printed and bound in Malaysia by
Times Offset (M) Sdn. Bnd.

Contents

Introduction 6
Getting Started 8

PROJECTS
1: Berries and Blossom Mirror 18
2: Daisy Chair 22
3: Ivy Kitchen Shelf 26
    Fruit Gallery 30
4: Rosebud Platter 32
5: Key Holder 36
6: Tulip Watering Can 40
    Garden Items Gallery 44
7: Rose Lamp 46
8: Antique "Leather" Writing Desk 50
9: Honeysuckle and Blossom Tray 54
10: Country Chest 58
11: Italian Marble Table 64
    Children's Nursery Gallery 68
12: Pansy Placemat and Coaster 70
13: Decorated Wall and Table 76
14: Crackle and Gold Leaf Waste-bin 80
15: Fuchsia Screen 84

Templates 90
Suppliers 95
Index 96

Introduction

Decorative painting is as old as mankind itself and the desire to adorn our living space is what makes us different from other species. From cave-dwellers and ancient Egyptians to present-day home improvers, people have been decorating their homes in one way or another for years as a means of stamping their individuality. Over the centuries many distinctive styles have evolved, some particular to specific countries or regions.

My first flirtation with decorative painting began many years ago. At the time, the range of products available was quite limited and my efforts often ended in frustration. By comparison, today's modern products are really easy to work with and the vast range for different uses is almost limitless, making the exciting world of decorative painting all the easier to achieve.

You do not have to be an expert artist to take up decorative painting and often the simplest designs are the most effective. Most modern day decorative painting is worked by tracing designs from books or pattern packs, which is a great way to get started. However, the satisfaction you will gain from creating something individual will inspire you to develop your skills. It is most definitely a learnable art form – the basic brushstrokes can be picked up and then grouped together in much the same way that we learn our alphabet as children and group the letters together to form words.

Decorative Painting for the Home is intended as a basic guide for the beginner who wants to learn this popular craft. The "Getting Started" section tells you everything you need to know about materials and equipment, preparing surfaces, transferring designs and basic painting techniques. The projects range in style from simple pieces, which are perfect for the complete beginner, such as the tulip watering can, to more challenging projects such as the beautiful floral screen. You will find all the inspiration and advice you need to create beautiful, original items for your home.

Happy painting!

Getting Started

Choosing items to paint

As with any hobby, it is possible to be overcome with enthusiasm and rush out and spend a fortune buying all sorts of equipment, paints and other items that you might never use. If you are a beginner you will need to experiment with a few simple projects to find out what you like doing and the best way of going about this is to hunt around the home for suitable things to paint.

The projects in this book cover a range of different surfaces – from wood and medium density fibreboard (MDF) to ceramics, metal and plastic. Waste-bins, trinket boxes, plant pots, lamp bases, hairbrush backs, chairs, stools and trays can all be transformed into wonderful painted items, and you will soon find yourself painting anything that doesn't move! Car boot sales and garage sales are ideal opportunities for finding "one-off" objects at give-away prices and you can often find bargains on market stalls. Don't be put off if something catches your eye but is the wrong colour or is already painted – with a little bit of preparation and a new coat of base colour you can create the perfect blank canvas for your ideas. Painting on thin card is a great way to practise smaller designs – why not make some greetings cards and gift tags? Family and friends will appreciate the fact that you have taken the time and care to create them a unique gift, rather than simply buying one.

There are many companies producing "blanks" in wood and MDF for decorating and these can vary from the simplest key ring and coaster shapes to intricate armoires. As you become more experienced, you will want to choose more interesting pieces to paint or perhaps move on to large-scale projects such as painting a wall in a room in your home. Painted screens are a great way of adding colour and a bit of fun to a room and, because they are movable, you can use them in different areas of the house as your mood changes.

BRUSHES

The old adage "A workman is only as good as his tools" is certainly true and it is far better to buy one or two good brushes designed especially for decorative painting, than to buy a whole handful of cheap or inappropriate brushes that will disappoint you. It always upsets me to see keen children given poor brushes, as even the youngest child values a good result and can be taught to use and care for a good brush from the start. Specialist brushes for decorative painters and folk artists have sharp chisel edges on flat brushes and sharp points on round brushes. They are designed to keep their shape well and will give good results. Buying the right brushes will pay off and eventually save you time, money and a lot of disappointment. A good brush can last a lifetime, or certainly decades, given the treatment and care that it deserves. The correct brushes need not be expensive, and you should start with a small number, adding to them as your need grows. With all the different brushes on the market it can be difficult to choose

the right brush for the job. Ideally, a good household brush, a round brush, a flat brush and a liner should satisfy your initial needs. Sets of brushes are often sold in packs, particularly the specialist "One-stroke" brushes – you may find that it is more economical to go for this option.

Brushes fall into two categories: natural hair or synthetic fibres. Synthetic brushes have a "spring" to the hairs and for the beginner, they are easier to use and care for than brushes made from natural hair. They are hardwearing, more reasonably priced and ideally suited to acrylic paints. These are some of the different types of brush you will come across in this book.

Household brushes
A 2.5 cm (1 in) good-quality flat brush is a good size for applying base colour to a number of items and will suit most of the projects in this book. Later you may wish to add a 2 cm (½ in) brush for painting smaller items, or an 8 cm (3 in) brush if you are venturing into decorating larger furniture. Buy the best brush you can afford, as an inferior brush will leave loose hairs on your work and ruin it.

Round brushes
The round brush is a relatively short brush, designed to a sharp point and fixed in a round metal ferrule. Better quality brushes even have tapered hairs to increase the sharpness of the tip. You will find round brushes in a variety of sizes, usually in sizes 1 to 12 (the lower the number, the smaller the brush). They are ideal for strokework, petals and leaves. They are also used for filling in and colourwashing small areas.

Flat brushes
Flat brushes have a flat metal ferrule, and are designed to end in a sharp chisel edge. They are used for filling in areas, floating and shading, and for some strokework (see page 15). You can paint on the flat side or the chisel edge when a fine line is needed.

Liner brushes
A liner brush is a long, thin, round brush tapered to a gradual point at the tip. It is used for outlining, or for long thin lines such as stems, stalks, tendrils or curlicues (see page 16). A shorter liner is known as a detail brush or spotter. These are easier for

This set of "One-stroke" brushes is made up of flat brushes. From left to right: No.1 Script, Liner, No.2 Flat, No.6 Flat, Small Scruffy, Scruffy, ¾ Flat, No.12 Flat, No.10 Flat, No.8 Flat.

the beginner to control than a longer liner, and are used for minute details.

Stencil brushes

A stencil or stippling brush is a round brush with shorter, stiffer hairs in a round ferrule. They have short, stubby handles. They are used for pouncing, stencilling and stippling. Smaller brushes are useful for painting the centres of flowers or adding rosy cheeks to painted figures.

Scruffy brush

A scruffy brush is a stubby brush, designed to be used dry for pouncing or stippling. It is used for snow, wisteria-type flowers, moss etc. It is usually oval and generally softer than a stencil brush.

Sponge brush

These are a useful and inexpensive alternative for applying base colour and varnishes. They are disposable but, if cared for, have a limited lifespan.

Specialist brushes

In addition to the basic brushes detailed above you will find a whole range of other specialist brushes in every shape imaginable, from fan-shaped to angled brushes. These are not essential for a beginner and your specialist supplier can advise you as the need arises (see page 95 for a list of stockists and suppliers).

Brush care

A good-quality brush, if properly cared for, will last a lifetime. Always wash the size or dressing out of a new brush before using it. The size protects the brush during its long journey from manufacturer to artist. Always clean brushes immediately after using them with acrylics, in a jar of clean water. If you don't, the dried paint will "set" in the base of the hairs and splay your brush, thereby ruining it. Follow this with a wash in warm (not hot) water and mild soap or washing-up liquid. Continue until there is no colour at all when the brush is wiped on a paper towel.

Never leave brushes standing in a jar of water, as the hairs will bend and the shape of the brush is ruined. If this happens accidentally you can try and resurrect your brush by dipping the hair part briefly in hot water and reshaping the brush. Take care not to let the metal ferrule of a brush stand in hot water as the glue could melt and your brush fall apart. Brushes left standing in water can also be ruined if the wooden handles swell and split and the ferrules become loose. Fo this reason, more companies are now switching to plastic or acrylic handles.

Store your brushes standing handle down in an empty jar, or lying in a tray lined with paper towel. If you are travelling with your brushes, invest in a purpose-made brush carrier, available at art stores. This protects the delicate bristles from damage. Never store brushes away wet, as they could go mouldy. If you know that you are not using your brushes again for some time, you can "dress" the bristles with hair conditioner and allow them to dry. This will help protect and condition them, but they will need rinsing out before they are used again.

If you venture into painting with products that are not water-based, then you will need to use an appropriate product for cleaning your brushes. For example, use turpentine or white spirit to clean brushes used with oil paint.

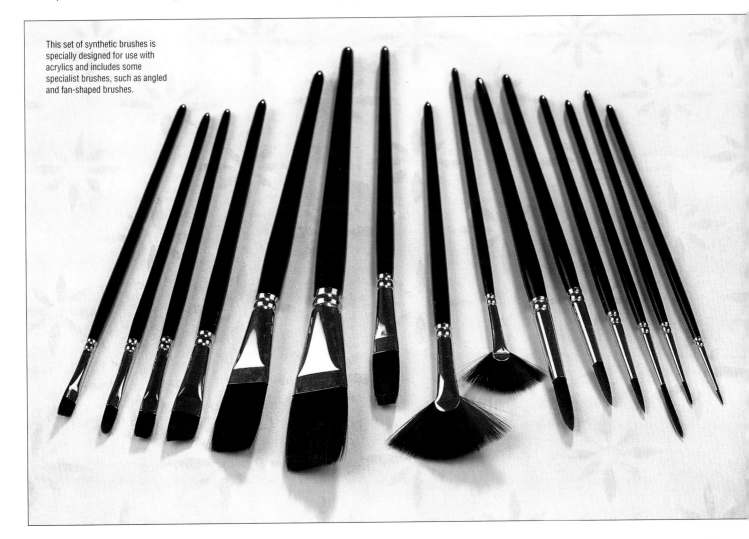

This set of synthetic brushes is specially designed for use with acrylics and includes some specialist brushes, such as angled and fan-shaped brushes.

PAINT

There are so many diverse products on the market that the choice can be bewildering for the beginner. Most of the projects in this book are painted using acrylic paints and I would always steer the beginner decorative artist towards acrylics for their first adventure. Acrylic paints can be used straight from the tube or bottle, are available in hundreds of colours, and can be mixed with water. They dry quickly, are odourless and economical, and you can overpaint your mistakes easily. They are just the right consistency for applying base colour and stroke work. Brushes can be cleaned in soap and water and acrylic paint

spills can be removed from clothing if tackled while still wet.

In addition to the actual acrylic paints, you will find there are a few other products that you will find useful. A wide range of mediums are available that adapt acrylic paint to make it suitable for fabric, ceramic and tiles or glassware. There are others that alter the finish to glitter or pearlized, or simply make it flow more easily or dry more slowly. Once a project is complete, it is a good idea to seal it in some way and a couple of coats of varnish will protect your work and make your items more hardwearing, as well as enhance the colours. It is available in different finishes and can sprayed from a can or brushed on. Keep a brush specifically for varnishing so it is not soiled with paint. Most manufacturers produce comprehensive free leaflets on their paint and mediums and wonderful websites full of product information, projects, colour charts, technical data and details of suppliers for mail order for those not living near a store (see page 95).

OTHER USEFUL EQUIPMENT

Most of the other things you will need to get started you will probably already have in your home.

Water pot
You can buy water pots specifically designed to hold a number of paintbrushes while you work but a clean jam jar works just as well. Remember to change the water occasionally.

Palettes
A ceramic tile makes a good palette for dispensing paint on to and is easy to clean. I use waxed palette paper, available in pads. The advantage of palette paper is that you can blend on it – it is also inexpensive and disposable. In warmer climates, it is often necessary to use a "wet palette". A wet palette consists of a layer of palette paper over a wet sponge layer in a plastic tray. You will find them in art stores, or you can improvise by making your own. They stop the paint from drying too quickly on the palette and if you cover them, you can preserve the same paint palette for a longer period until your project is complete.

Palette knife
A small palette knife is useful for mixing paint; never mix paint with a paintbrush as this ruins them.

Sponges
Both natural sea sponges and pieces of synthetic sponge can be used to create a sponged effect, particularly over a large area. Natural sponges have a more open texture and, because they are irregular, will produce a more interesting pattern. See page 17 for sponging techniques

Cotton buds
Cotton buds are ideal for applying paint in the form of dots or highlights. They are also useful for removing mistakes cleanly.

Cocktail sticks
These are useful for applying small amounts of glue and can also be used instead of a stylus to create very small dots.

Masking tape
Low-tack tape can be used to cover areas that you don't want painted to create bold designs and clean lines. You can also use it to tape traced designs or stencils on to your work.

Stylus
This versatile tool is ideal for tracing over templates in order to transfer designs, although a sharp pencil makes a good substitute. The stylus is also useful for creating small dots (see page 17).

Tracing paper and transfer paper
These are essential for transferring templates and designs on to blank objects

Paper towel
A useful kitchen item that comes in particularly handy when mopping up accidental spills! It is also useful for wiping your paintbrushes.

Sanding pad or sandpaper
Preparing your items before painting is an essential part of the process. Wood or MDF (medium density fibreboard) items will need to be sanded, depending on how rough the surface is. Take care when sanding MDF items – either wear a mask or work outdoors.

BASIC TECHNIQUES

Preparation

Always prepare your surface well, as this is the key to success. If you skimp this stage, you will regret it later and often spoil the end result. Sand and seal new blanks before painting, and ensure you wash and dry old items to remove dirt and grease from the surface. Sand down old paint to give a smooth surface that provides a "key" to your painting. Metal and glass items benefit from a wipe over with a 50:50 solution of vinegar and water. Unless you like the distressed look, always fill the smallest holes in wood with wood filler. Remember to prepare the back, underside, and inside of all items as this prevents warping and gives a well-finished look.

Sandpaper comes in a whole range of grades, from the very fine to very coarse. Wet-and-dry sandpaper can be used wet and sanding pads are excellent as they allow you to apply even pressure to all areas. If you are sanding large areas of MDF, it is advisable to wear a mask.

The base coat of colour should be applied with a good-quality flat brush or foam brush, using as large a brush as possible for the job in hand. A few thin coats give a far better finish than one heavy coat. Sand down the surface after each coat dries and polish with a brown paper bag.

LEARNING THE STROKES

The best way to get the basic strokes right is to practise, practise, practise! Keep scraps of paper or card nearby when you work so you can run through the strokes before you attempt to paint the piece that you are working on. Remember as well that there are very few mistakes that can't be corrected!

Loading a flat brush with paint and medium

When using a flat brush, only load the brush with paint about three-quarters of the way up the bristles. The side of the brush is dipped first into the small "puddle" of medium and then the other side is dipped into the colour. Pull the brush along the paper using the full width of the brush to create a path of colour – this is known as blending.

Loading a flat brush with two colours

The principle for loading a brush with two colours, known as double-loading, is the same as for loading a brush with paint and medium. Dip the bristles of one corner of a flat brush into the first colour of paint. Load the opposite corner of the brush with the second colour. Blend the two colours by pulling the brush along the paper a few times until the colour start to merge – you will start to see a "third" colour appearing.

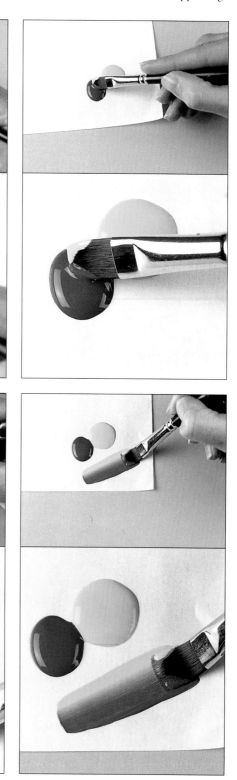

Tipping a round brush

Tipping is when you basically load a brush with one colour but then dip the point of it into a second colour. This gives a highlight to the strokes, especially when working comma strokes.

giving you light and shade in one stroke. Larger leaves may need two strokes to fill them. Complete half of the leaf and then repeat overlapping onto the first half. The double-loaded colours will create a vein effect down the centre of the leaf.

Creating "C" strokes with a flat brush

"C" strokes (which can also be "U" strokes, depending on the direction) are wonderful for filling in curved shapes such as petals. Choose a brush size to suit the design. You will need to hold the brush upright while working this stroke. Apply the chisel edge of the brush to the surface and slide one side a short distance using just the thin chisel edge. Continue into a curve and apply pressure using the whole width of the brush. As you complete the curve, release the pressure and end on the thin chisel edge again, parallel to where you started. This can really only be completed in one action. Double-loading the brush increases the effect and adds realism.

Creating "S" strokes with a flat brush

"S" strokes are perfect for creating leaves. Load the brush with paint and start with the brush upright and perpendicular to the surface. Place the chisel edge down and apply pressure while drawing towards you, ending on the chisel edge (parallel to where you started). Double-load the brush in two colours for more realistic leaves,

Creating a comma stroke

Probably the most widely used stroke, this is a tip, press and lift stroke. Load your brush and lay the brush tip down. Apply pressure allowing the brush to spread, pull the brush along the paper, gently lifting as you go. End the stroke on the tip of the brush only, forming the tail of the comma stroke. Practise them upright, leaning to the left and right, and in all sizes. This stroke is useful for petals, filling in leaves and for border decoration. Tipping the brush in a second colour gives colour gradation to your strokes.

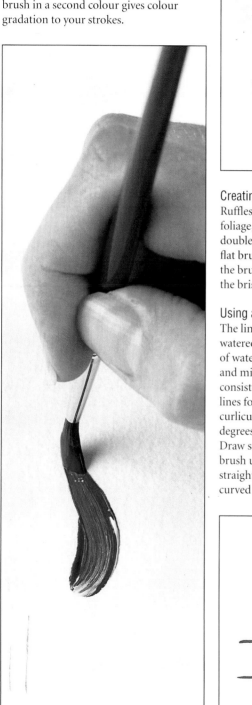

Creating a "ruffle"

Ruffles are fun to do and are great for foliage, especially when the brush is double-loaded with two colours. Using a flat brush, apply pressure to the "heel" of the brush and then "wiggle" the brush so the bristles fan out.

Using a liner brush

The liner brush is used with slightly watered-down paint. Just add a few drops of water to bottled paint on your palette and mix until you have an inky consistency. Practise straight and curved lines for stems and veins and tendrils and curlicues. Keep the liner brush at 90 degrees to your surface for easier curves. Draw stems using a liner brush or flat brush up on its chisel edge. Avoid stiff straight stems as much as possible – curved lines look much more realistic.

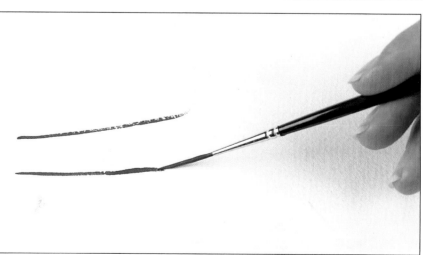

Dots

Dots are useful for filler flowers, pollen on larger flowers and for patterns and borders. They can be made using the wooden end of a thin paintbrush or with a stylus. For dots of a uniform size, dip the brush end or stylus into the paint each time. If you do a few dots before reloading you will notice that the size of each dot reduces as the amount of paint diminishes.

Sponging

Sponging is effective on walls and for backgrounds. A natural sea sponge gives the most interesting effects due to the open, textured surface. Always practise on paper to achieve the look you want and rotate the sponge so that you do not get a repetitive design. Double-load the sponge with more than one colour, or sponge with one colour, dry, and add a subsequent different colour layer.

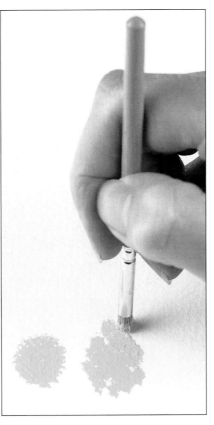

Stippling

Stippling is a pouncing action. It makes useful backgrounds, realistic looking lilac and wisteria flowers and is also used in stencilling and faux finishes. Use a purpose-made stippling brush, or a stencil brush or any shorthaired stiff bristle brush. Practise light and heavy stippling and experiment with more than one colour. Stippling is also good for creating flower centres and rosy cheeks on painted figures.

DESIGN INSPIRATION

There are a plethora of design books and pattern packs on the market and these can be resized easily to fit your projects, by scanning and reprinting on your computer, or by reduction, enlargement or reversal on a photocopying machine.

You can also adapt embroidery patterns or designs from your other crafts. Children's colouring books and clip art are also valuable sources. You will soon be enjoying designing your own patterns. Always be careful not to infringe other people's copyright.

Tracing

As we have already mentioned, most decorative painters start by working from tracings of pre-prepared designs and so a pad of good quality, A4 size, tracing paper is a must. You can use rolls of greaseproof paper from a food store, but many painters prefer the A4-sized tracing paper as you can hand-feed this into your computer printer and print off the tracing from a scanned design.

Transfer paper

Artists' transfer paper is paper coated with either chalk or graphite and can be used several times. The transfer paper is placed between the traced design and the base coated surface with the chalk or graphite side facing down. Going over the design with a stylus or an empty ballpoint pen transfers the design. Use the chalk transfer paper on dark surfaces and the graphite version on light surfaces so that your design will show up more easily. Never use typing carbon paper, as this will mark your work with ugly smears that cannot be removed.

Painting groups

Many areas have decorative painting and folk art groups, and joining one is a great way to make friends with people of similar interests. A decorative painting group provides an opportunity to swap ideas, attend product demonstrations and invite in guest artists to teach new techniques.

Berries and Blossom Mirror

This lovely berries and blossom mirror gives beginners the opportunity to practise the basic strokes while achieving a professional result. The design can easily be adapted to suit a range of painting surfaces.

1 Seal the mirror by covering the glass with a square of paper and spraying the frame lightly with spray sealer. Trace the blackberries design on page 91 and transfer the design on to the mirror frame by placing the transfer paper under the tracing and going over the design with a stylus or sharp pencil.

You will need

Hauser dark green

titanium white

primary blue

deep burgundy

lemon yellow

lamp black

light avocado

Small pine mirror, 26 cm (10 in) square

Acrylic matt sealer/finisher

Tracing paper

Grey transfer paper

Stylus or sharp pencil

Acrylic paints, such as DecoArt Americana, as shown above

Size 5 round brush

Cotton buds

Detail brush

Small flat brush

Angle shader brush

Liner brush

2 Paint the large leaves using five comma strokes and a size 5 round brush, loading the brush in Hauser dark green tipped in titanium white.

3 Paint the single leaves using single comma strokes. Use the same brush but this time use only the Hauser dark green paint.

4 Paint the individual drupelets of the berries using a cotton bud dipped in primary blue, and a pouncing action. Practise on paper first. Do not overload the cotton bud. You should get a print with a lighter area in the middle. This mimics the bloom of the fruit. Paint the outer circle first, keeping the fruit irregular and realistic, then fill in the centre. While the paint is still wet, add some dabs of deep burgundy to one third of each berry, to the right hand side. Add a tiny white highlight with the titanium white paint and a detail brush to most drupelets.

5 Paint the blossoms in titanium white. Water down the paint for a translucent look. Use the small flat brush and a "C" stroke for each petal. Fill in the centre with lemon yellow, using a cotton bud. Add some pollen dots with lamp black paint and a stylus.

6 Add sprays of filler leaves using a small angle brush and a watery mix of light avocado. Use the liner brush to add a few curly tendrils in the same colour. Do the tendrils freehand, as this is easier than trying to follow a traced line. Finish with a few filler groups of three dots in titanium white paint using the stylus.

7 Allow to dry and finish with spray sealer/finisher, remembering to protect the glass area with paper again.

variation

A hairbrush back provides a good surface for painting. You may need to re-size an element of the design to fit your chosen item.

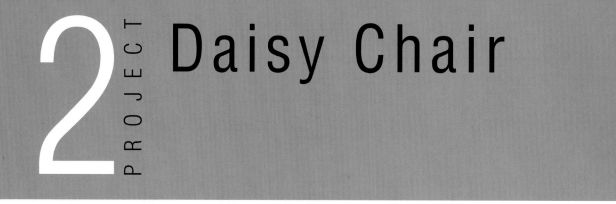

Daisy Chair

F resh as a daisy, this design will delight the youngest
member of any family, whilst being robust and functional.
Plastic plays an important part in our lives and with modern
specialist paints you can now paint on to plastic without the
paint cracking or peeling off.

1 Wipe over the entire surface of the chair with a cloth dampened with rubbing alcohol. This removes static charge and any film left from when the plastic was moulded. Allow to dry.

You will need

hunter green

neon green

white

yellow

black

Plastic child's chair

Rubbing alcohol

Tracing paper

White transfer paper

Stylus or sharp pencil

Paint for plastic, such as Plaid's, as shown above

Medium flat brush

Size 5 round brush

Small stippling brush

Small flat brush

Kneadable artist's eraser

Sealant

2 Trace the daisy design on page 91 and then transfer the pattern on to the back by placing the transfer paper under the tracing and going over the design with a stylus or sharp pencil. The bud design should be traced on to the seat.

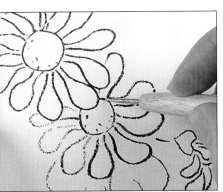

3 Double-load a medium-sized flat brush with hunter green and
neon green and paint the larger leaves in two strokes. Work from
the base of the leaf to the tip, keeping the neon green to the middle
of the leaf. Leave to dry for about 10 minutes.

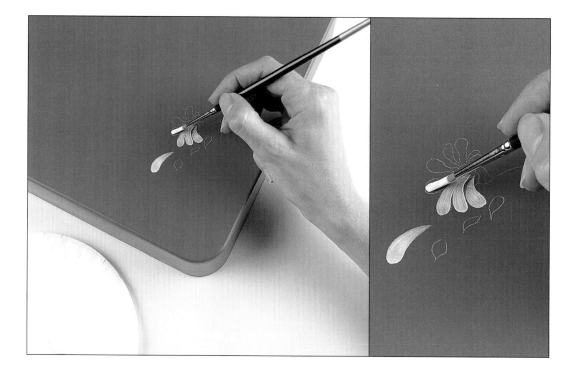

4 Load a size 5 round brush with white paint and paint the petals on
both the back and seat of the chair using comma strokes.
Complete all the petals, except any that overlap the flower centre.

5 Take the stippling brush and pounce it into the yellow paint to load the brush. Do a few tests on paper first and then, using a pouncing action, fill each flower centre with yellow. Leave to dry before adding any remaining white petals that overlap the yellow centres.

6 Using the small flat brush, paint in the small leaves and calyxes in neon green. Pull in the stem using the chisel edge of the brush and then leave to dry – this should take about 10 minutes.

7 Add a crescent of pollen dots to the lower half of the flower centres, using black paint and the stylus. For dots of a uniform size you will have to reload the stylus after each dot. Allow to cure for 3 weeks before removing any chalk marks that are showing through the design using a kneadable artist's eraser. Coat the chair with a paint for plastic sealant for added protection and water resistance.

3 PROJECT Ivy Kitchen Shelf

Stephanie Weightman

This pine shelf was a junk shop find that was already stained green. Here the antique look has been enhanced by using a distressing technique: candle wax was rubbed into the wood and then the shelf was painted with a watery mix of white acrylic paint for a limewashed effect, with some areas left whiter than others. Grapes and vines trail across the top of the shelf and down the sides – perfect for a country-style kitchen.

You will need

green forest
wicker white
berry wine
midnight

Pine shelf unit
Acrylic paints, such as FolkArt, as shown above
Size 12 one-stroke flat brush
Liner brush
Gilding cream in classic gold

1 Make sure that the surface you are working on is smooth, clean and dry. Double-load the size 12 flat brush with green forest and wicker white and, working on the chisel edge, paint in the vines, leading with the lighter colour. Criss-cross the vines for a more natural effect. It is best to work freehand but do use the drawing on page 92 as a guide.

2 Add the grapes with a double-load of berry wine and midnight on the flat brush. Place the brush down on the chisel edge and rotate the brush to form a complete circle. Paint some grapes with midnight to the centre and some with berry wine to the centre. Add a white highlight to each grape with a liner brush, keeping the highlight in the same position on each grape.

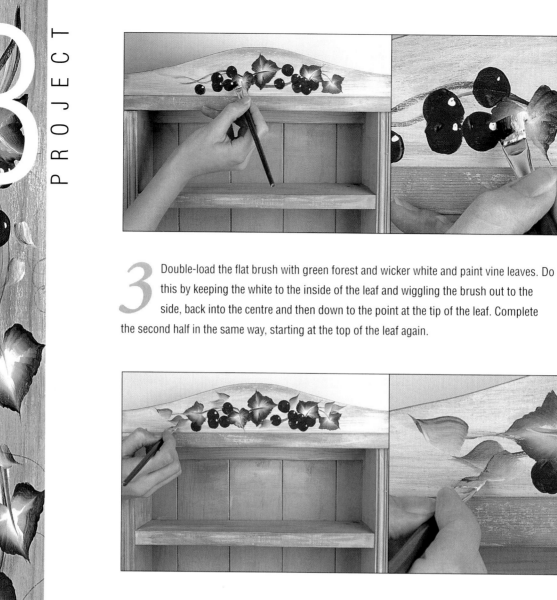

3 Double-load the flat brush with green forest and wicker white and paint vine leaves. Do this by keeping the white to the inside of the leaf and wiggling the brush out to the side, back into the centre and then down to the point at the tip of the leaf. Complete the second half in the same way, starting at the top of the leaf again.

4 Add the smaller one-stroke leaves with the flat brush double-loaded in green forest and wicker white. You can change the size of the flat brush to a smaller brush if you wish or use the size 12 throughout.

5 Mix green forest paint with water until you have an inky consistency. Using the liner brush, add a few tendrils curling in and out of the leaves.

6 Rub the distressed areas with gilding cream for an antique effect. The best way to apply gilding cream is with your finger.

artist's tip
Thinning the paint with water until you have an inky consistency makes tendril painting and other fine liner work much easier.

Fruit
Gallery

Utensil holder
A whole harvest of fruits, painted
on to galvanized ware using
FolkArt acrylic paints. The design
is by Priscilla Hauser.

Gooseberry tray
This delicate gooseberry design
on a smoked marbleized
background was painted by artist
Liz Bramhall. The technique uses
the smoke from a candle flame.

Pear trough
This trough was painted by Priscilla
Hauser using FolkArt acrylic paints
in an unusual design of pears and
chequerboard. The resulting effect
is dynamic and fresh.

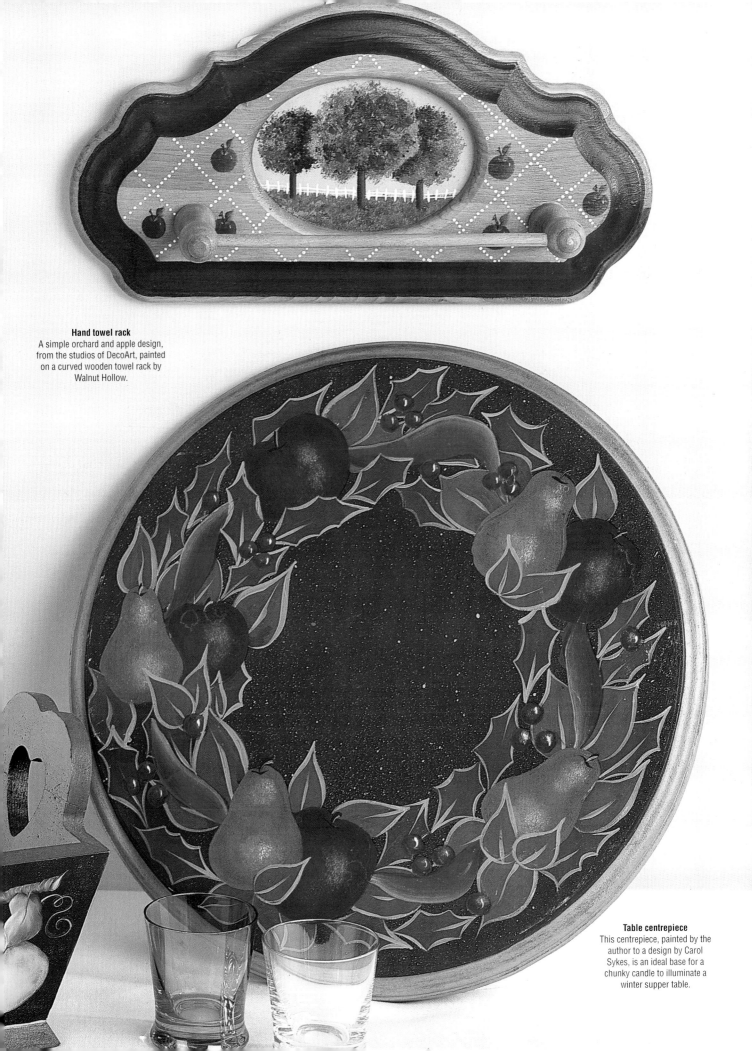

Hand towel rack
A simple orchard and apple design, from the studios of DecoArt, painted on a curved wooden towel rack by Walnut Hollow.

Table centrepiece
This centrepiece, painted by the author to a design by Carol Sykes, is an ideal base for a chunky candle to illuminate a winter supper table.

4 PROJECT Rosebud Platter

Carol Sykes

This pretty rosebud platter uses the classic "One-stroke" painting technique, developed by Donna Dewbury in the United States. The design is simple and elegant, making it a perfect project for a beginner. Try practising the more complex elements of the design on paper until you have perfected them.

1 Using the soft 2.5 cm (1 in) brush, apply a base coat of silver sage green to the whole platter. Leave to dry before sanding gently with a fine grade sandpaper and then apply a second coat of silver sage green. Apply the metallic glorious gold paint to the rim of the platter using the size 8 flat brush. When it is completely dry, use the sandpaper to rub back the gold, creating a distressed finish.

You will need

silver sage green
metallic glorious gold
evergreen
titanium white
cranberry wine

MDF oval platter
Acrylic paints, such as DecoArt Americana, as shown above
2.5 cm (1 in) soft flat brush
Fine sandpaper
Size 8 flat brush
Tracing paper
Grey transfer paper
Stylus or sharp pencil
Liner brush
Size 10 flat brush
Soft eraser
Clear satin varnish

2 Trace the rosebud design on page 90. Transfer the design on to the platter by placing the transfer paper under the tracing and going over the design with a stylus or sharp pencil.

3 Load the size 8 flat brush with evergreen paint and paint the smaller leaves using an "S" stroke. Double-load the size 10 flat brush with evergreen and titanium white and paint the larger leaves using "S" strokes.

4 Double-load the size 8 flat brush with cranberry wine and titanium white and paint the rosebuds. These are made up of two "C" strokes.

5 Using the liner brush loaded with evergreen, paint in the stems to all the leaves and buds. Paint in the calyx for each bud and then some tendrils. Load the liner brush with titanium white paint and apply three dots to the centre of each bud.

6 Double-load the size 10 flat brush with cranberry wine and titanium white. Paint the roses following the design – you may want to practise a few on paper before you start painting on the platter. (See below for how the strokes are made.) Using the tip of the liner brush loaded with titanium white paint, apply dots to the centre of each rose, as well as some areas of white dots around the design.

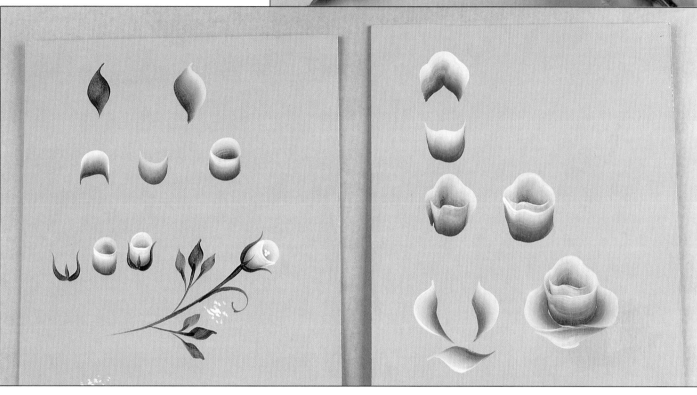

7 When the platter is completely dry, use a soft eraser to remove any traced lines. Apply two coats of satin varnish, allowing plenty of drying time between each coat.

5 PROJECT

Key Holder

Paula Haley

This delightful key holder, painted with chrysanthemums and tulips, gives you another chance to practise your comma strokes and use some "S" strokes. This project, with its vibrant colours, will make a real statement for your home, while making sure that you never lose your keys!

1 If your key holder comes with hooks, remove them before sanding gently. Apply a base coat in yellow ochre with the flat brush and allow to dry before applying a second coat. Trace the design on page 92 and transfer on to the key holder by placing the transfer paper under the tracing and going over the design with a stylus or sharp pencil.

2 To paint the long leaves, load the size 5 round brush with avocado tipped with Hauser light green. Use elongated "S" strokes to paint the leaves. Then using the same technique and brush, paint the three fatter leaves under the chrysanthemum with avocado tipped with cadmium yellow.

You will need

yellow ochre
avocado
Hauser light green
cadmium yellow
burgundy wine
burnt umber
titanium white
cadmium orange
cranberry wine
true red
sapphire

MDF or wooden key holder
Sanding pad
Acrylic paints, such as DecoArt Americana, as shown above
2.5 cm (1 in) flat brush
Tracing paper
Grey transfer paper
Stylus or sharp pencil
Size 5 round brush
Long liner brush
Size 4 round brush
Water-based varnish

3 Apply a base coat of burgundy wine to the main flower ball of the chrysanthemum using comma strokes. Give the ball of the flower a second coat, adding a touch of burnt umber to the burgundy wine for depth.

4 Load the size 5 brush with burgundy wine tipped with titanium white and paint the petals of the flower using comma strokes. Add dabs of pollen to the bowl of the flower with the same brush and paint, and soften.

5 Apply a base coat to the tulips using cadmium orange and the size 5 round brush. Use elongated "S" strokes. Then paint the petals with cranberry wine tipped with true red. Paint the two outside petals first, then add the central petal. Add a comma stroke to each outside petal using the same brush loaded with cadmium orange, tipped with titanium white.

6 Using slightly thinned avocado paint and a long liner brush, paint in the stems of the long filler flowers at the sides of the design. Load the size 4 round brush with sapphire tipped with titanium white and add tiny buds using small comma strokes. Work down the stem from the tip. Using the same brush and paint, add small flowers around the chrysanthemum using small dab strokes. Add a dot centre using cadmium yellow and a stylus.

7 Load the size 4 round brush with avocado tipped with titanium white and add clusters of three comma strokes. Thin a little avocado paint with water until you have an inky consistency and add a few tendrils with the liner brush. Allow to cure for 24 hours before applying two coats of water-based varnish.

PROJECT

Tulip Watering Can

Ann Myers

unctional items do not need to be boring and can be decorated to match your home. This tall elegant watering can for houseplants has been given a new look. The sage-green colour goes well with your plants and will suit most colour schemes. The simple tulip design gives you a chance to practise your basic strokes.

You will need

teal green

desert turquoise

primary blue

antique gold

Metal watering can,
approximately 23 cm (9 in) tall

Soft cloth

Vinegar

No-prep metal paint in sage green

Large flat brush

Tracing paper

White transfer paper

Stylus or pencil

Acrylic paints, such as DecoArt
Americana, as shown above

Size 5 round brush

Liner brush

Size 2 round brush

Acrylic spray sealer/finisher
(optional)

1 Wipe over the metal watering can with a cloth dampened with a 50:50 solution of vinegar and water. This removes any grease from the metal.

2 Apply a base coat to the body of the watering can with a large flat brush and the sage green metal paint. Leave the spout and handle unpainted or, if you wish, cover the whole area. Leave to dry for about one hour and then apply a second coat.

3 When the watering can is dry, trace the tulip design on page 94 and transfer the design on to the watering can by placing the transfer paper under the tracing and going over the design with the stylus or pencil.

4 Paint the base petals of the tulip head in teal green acrylic paint, using a size 5 round brush and a comma stroke, then paint in the stem. Using the same brush, paint the bottom leaf, to the right-hand side of the stem, using teal green and a comma stroke. Paint the leaf above, adding a little desert turquoise. Continue working upwards, painting each leaf above and adding a little desert turquoise paint to the brush each time to give a gradation of colour.

5 Add the two side petals to the head of the tulip in desert turquoise, using the size 5 round brush and a comma stroke for each petal. Paint the petals to the left-hand side of the stem using the same method as for the other side, starting with primary blue and adding progressive amounts of desert turquoise as you proceed up the stem.

6 Fill in the centre petal of the tulip with three comma strokes, using the size 5 brush and primary blue. Using the liner brush, add curly tendrils around the leaves and stem with a watery mix of antique gold. Complete the design by adding small comma strokes on to the centre petal using a size 2 round brush and antique gold paint. Leave to dry.

variation

A plant pot trimmed with the same galvanized metal can be painted to match the watering can.

artist's tip

Although the no-prep metal doesn't need a sealer, a light spray will protect the design.

Garden Items
Gallery

Butterfly house and bird house
These two boxes are made from
simple plywood. They have been
painted with patio paint and
decorated with freehand designs.

Small watering can
This tin watering can was painted with no-prep
metal paint before being decorated with a
simple floral design using comma strokes.

Plant pot
A flower pot was given a base coat of strong
blue paint to resemble sky. The clouds and
greenery have been sponged and stippled, while
the bird boxes have been painted freehand.

Foxglove watering can
This simple watering can, painted by Ann Myers, has a lovely design of foxgloves. The flowers are painted using "C" strokes.

Fuchsia watering can
You can adapt and transfer most designs on to any surface – the fuchsia design on this watering can is similar to the one on pages 84–89.

Scalloped-edge pot
This terracotta pot was painted with cream patio paint and then decorated with love birds and a border of comma strokes in lilac and turquoise.

7 Rose Lamp

Stephanie Weightman

F loral designs are always popular and these huge roses in
shades of pink will brighten up a bedroom. Practise
painting the roses before you begin – you will soon see how
easy it is to achieve wonderful results!

You will need

wicker white

berry wine

hot pink

thicket

hunter green

basil green

Inca gold

Lamp base, approximately 30 cm (12 in) high

Acrylic paints, such as FolkArt, as shown above

2 cm (¾ in) one-stroke flat brush

Sheet of clear acetate

Size 12 one-stroke flat brush

Acrylic spray sealer

1 Apply a base coat in wicker white to the whole of the base of the lamp using the flat brush. Allow to dry.

2 Photocopy or trace the petal shapes on page 93. Place the acetate sheet over the shapes and use this as a practice worksheet before you start painting the lamp. You can paint directly on to the acetate – simply wipe it clean and start again. Double-load the 2 cm (¾ in) brush with white and either berry wine or hot pink. Blend the colours on the brush and practise the strokes as follows: to paint the large petals, start with the brush on the chisel edge of the left-hand side of the petal, press down on the brush and wiggle the brush in a fan shape until the petal is filled, ending on the right-hand side on the chisel edge. Use two "C" strokes to create the rose centre, reversing the second one. Use comma strokes to create side petals.

3 Paint the roses randomly over the lamp using wicker white and one of the flower colours for each rose. Vary the colours from rose to rose. Wipe any excess paint from your brush when changing colour, but do not wash the brush out when starting another colour flower, as a little of one flower colour left in the brush helps harmonize the flowers.

4 Using the acetate sheet, practise painting the rose leaves. Double-load the 2 cm (¾ in) flat brush with thicket and wicker white. Starting on the chisel edge and, with the white to the centre of the leaf, wiggle the brush in a fan shape, bringing the brush round to a point. Repeat on the other side to complete the leaf. Remember to leave room for the medium- and smaller-sized leaves.

artist's tip

Using a sheet of acetate to practise your strokes is a great way of perfecting your skills and building up confidence. The acetate can be cleaned with a damp cloth, and reused.

5 Add random medium-sized one-stroke leaves with a size 12 flat brush, using a blend of hunter green and wicker white for some, and a blend of basil green and wicker white for others. Remember to leave room for the small gold leaves.

6 Using the size 12 flat brush and Inca gold paint, fill in any spaces with smaller single stroke leaves. Allow to dry.

variation

Decorate a plain white lampshade to match the base. You can keep the same paints and colours but keep the design to a minimum – a simple border echoes elements of the main design but is not too overpowering.

7 Protect the surface of the lamp by spraying it with a coat of acrylic spray sealer.

8 PROJECT

Antique "Leather" Writing Desk

The technique of using tissue paper to imitate leather is fun and easy to do and means that you can create elegant items, such as this tabletop writing desk, without spending a fortune. For a classic look, add a gold stencilled motif.

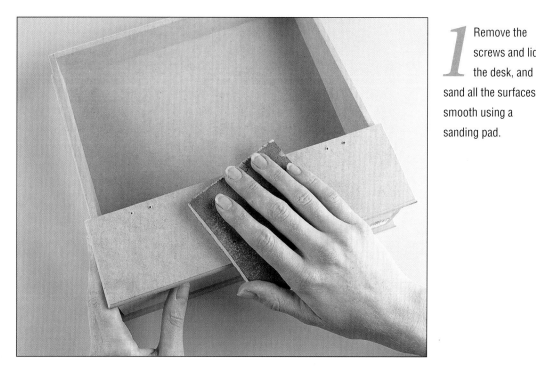

1 Remove the screws and lid of the desk, and sand all the surfaces smooth using a sanding pad.

2 Apply a base coat to the desk and lid, using lamp black acrylic paint and the large flat brush. Work in sections and allow to dry completely before applying a second coat. Set aside to dry.

3 Tear black tissue paper into small pieces, keeping the edges rough. Crumple them up in your hand and then smooth them out again, so that they are wrinkled. Prepare enough to cover the lid of the desk.

4 Using a flat brush, apply a coat of PVA adhesive to the top of the desk lid only.

5 Press the tissue paper on to the glued surface using a soft, clean, lint-free cloth. Use any straight edges along the sides and front of the lid and overlap the sheets at the top edge of the lid. Continue until the lid is completely covered, and allow to dry.

6 Using the large, flat brush, apply a coat of deep burgundy acrylic paint, mixed with a little extender medium, over the tissued surface and allow to dry. For a more aged appearance, rub back the deep burgundy with a clean, damp cloth to allow some of the black to show through. Leave to dry.

7 Paint the rest of the desk with deep burgundy paint. Use light, streaky strokes so that some of the black surface shows through.

8 Seal the lid of the desk with some spray sealer and allow to dry. Spray again and, when dry, buff the surface with a soft cloth for a durable finish. If you wish, apply a stencil decoration to the desk, using a self-adhesive stencil and a metallic gold pen.

variation

Use the same technique to make an attractive pen holder for your desktop.

Honeysuckle and Blossom Tray

Cynthia Horsfield

W hat better way to brighten up your morning than with a cup of tea served on this delightful tray. The honeysuckle and blossom design is pretty and delicate and could be used to decorate a whole range of items for the home.

1 Sand the tray, if necessary and then seal with the multi-purpose sealer. Apply a base coat in eggshell and leave to dry. Using masking tape, mark out the areas to be sponged – you need to create four triangles at the corners of the tray by placing masking tape from centre edge to centre edge. Load the sponge with antique mauve and sponge quickly and evenly. Allow to dry, then sponge with celery green.

2 Trace the honeysuckle and blossom design on page 93. Transfer the pattern on to the tray by placing the transfer paper under the traced design and going over the design with a stylus or sharp pencil.

You will need

eggshell
antique mauve
celery green
French vanilla
cadmium yellow
deep burgundy
avocado
white wash
antique gold
metallic glorious gold

MDF tray, 33 x 43 cm (13 x 17 in)
Sandpaper
Multi-purpose sealer
Acrylic paints, such as DecoArt Americana, as shown above
Large flat brush
Masking tape
Natural sponge
Tracing paper
Grey transfer paper
Stylus or sharp pencil
Size 5 round brush
Liner brush
Size 6 flat brush
Stippling brush
Cocktail stick
Clear varnish

3 Start to paint the honeysuckle flowers, using the size 5 round brush loaded with French vanilla and tipped with cadmium yellow. Paint the five large petals, using comma strokes. Load the brush with French vanilla tipped with deep burgundy and paint the three remaining smaller petals.

4 Using the liner brush and avocado paint, paint in the honeysuckle stems. Load the round brush with avocado and then side-load with cadmium yellow to paint the honeysuckle leaves. Using two strokes, begin at the stem and finish at the tip.

5 To paint the blossom design, start with the leaves. Double-load the size 6 flat brush with avocado and French vanilla and paint the small leaves using "S" strokes. Paint the larger leaves using two strokes. Start at the stem and finish at the tip.

6 Paint the blossom petals using the flat brush. Double-load and blend with white wash and deep burgundy and, using a pivot stroke, complete the flowers and buds. Using the stippling brush, add the centres in antique gold, cadmium yellow and white wash. Complete the flowers by using a cocktail stick to add dots of cadmium yellow and white wash. Finish the buds and stems using the liner brush and avocado.

7 Complete the design by adding dots to the edge of the sponging using the stylus or sharp pencil and metallic glorious gold paint. Leave to dry and then finish with two coats of varnish.

Edging the sponged area with a line of metallic gold dots adds definition.

Country Chest

This multi-drawer chest is a great way to store all your bits and pieces so that it is functional as well as decorative. This is a project that children will be able to work on with supervision and the result might encourage them to keep their things tidy! If you are short of space, the chest can be wall-mounted.

1 Prepare the surface of the chest by sanding with a fine sanding block. Wipe away all dust with a clean lint-free cloth.

2 Place the chest on a sheet of scrap paper to protect your work surface, and then spray the chest with acrylic clear sealer. Allow to dry.

decorative painting for the home/project 10

3   Paint the main body of the chest with forest green paint, using the large flat brush.
Apply the paint smoothly and evenly, and allow to dry. Lightly sand the surface and
wipe clean again. Apply a second coat of forest green and allow to dry.

4   Spray the main part of the chest with clear acrylic spray sealer/finisher to give a
finished look and add a coat of protection.

5 Take the six drawers and draw on the simple lines freehand using a chalk pencil. Alternatively, you can trace the design from the templates on page 94 and transfer the design using grey transfer paper.

6 Using the stippling brush and a pouncing action, paint the sky areas and the pond in country blue. Allow to dry.

7 Continue to fill in all the other areas with the appropriate colours, following the design. Allow to dry.

8 Add the flowers by applying tiny dots in yellow light and titanium white with a stylus or sharp pencil. Vary the size of the dots. Leave to dry and then add a few grasses with a liner brush.

These 3-D animal shapes are available in good art and craft shops. Alternatively if you are a woodworker, try making your own shapes.

9 When the drawers are completely dry, spray them with sealer/finisher, for added protection. Add the 3-D animals or button fronts as desired, using good quality craft glue and a cocktail stick.

variation

All sorts of simple wooden items can be painted in the same theme, such as this pen holder.

artist's tips

Reload the stylus with acrylic paint each time for dots the same size. For dots of reducing size, only reload as required.

Always use spray products outdoors or in a well-ventilated area.

A cocktail stick is a good tool for applying small amounts of adhesive.

11 PROJECT Italian Marble Table

Stephanie Weightman

Faux marbling has been a popular substitute for real marble, since ancient times, and can be worked on all sorts of surfaces. It is of course much more economical, less heavy and so much fun to do!

1 Paint the tabletop with sealant and allow to dry. Using the flat brush, apply a base coat to the entire surface in licorice paint. Leave to dry before resanding the tabletop if necessary. Rub gently with brown paper to smooth the surface. Apply a coat of licorice to the legs and stem of the table only, and move to one side, as these are now complete.

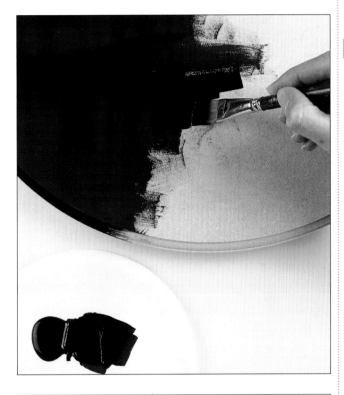

You will need

licorice

green forest

kelly green

Italian sage

wicker white

Small occasional table

Sealant

Acrylic paints, such as FolkArt, as shown above

2 cm (¾ in) flat brush

Sanding pad

Brown paper

Palette or paper plate

Extender

Natural sponge

Large natural badger hair brush

Long-haired script liner

Gloss varnish

2 Shake the paints. Squeeze some green forest paint on to your palette, in thin strings, randomly making circles and diagonals on the palette. Repeat with kelly green, making a lesser number of new circles and diagonals. Then add small amounts of Italian sage. Finally shake some drops of extender on the palette, over the colours already there. This is essential, as extender increases the drying time of the paints, giving you enough time to create your faux finish. Tilt the plate different ways to encourage the paints to move, but do not mix them.

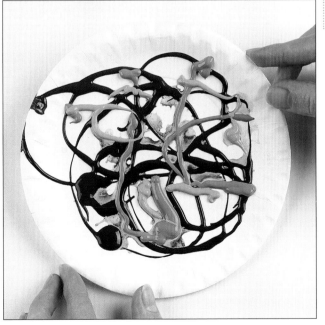

3 Load your natural sponge with paint by gently touching the sponge to the palette. Do not press down. Press the sponge lightly on to your tabletop, pick up, rotate the sponge, move to another area and repeat. Reload the sponge as needed. Continue until the tabletop and edges are complete, overlapping as you go. Leave some background colour showing and do not oversponge.

4 Soften the effect by gently brushing over the surface with a real badger hair brush while the paint is still wet. Leave to dry for at least two hours.

5 On a clean palette add some extender to a small amount of wicker white paint. Do not mix. Drag a longhaired script liner through this mixture and start to add the veining to your tabletop. Holding the brush at the end of the handle to give a loose quivering action, drag and pull the vein across the surface. Veins should be irregular and running in one direction, although not parallel, to look natural. Take care not to overdo it. Soften the vein effect by brushing gently over the veins with the badger brush. Leave to dry for 24 hours.

artist's tips

Always sand items made from Medium Density Fibreboard (MDF) outdoors, or in a well-ventilated area, and always wear a face mask, to protect your health.

Brown wrapping paper or paper bags make a great substitute for fine sandpaper, and give a wonderfully smooth surface.

6 Sand lightly if necessary, and smooth with a brown paper bag. Wipe away any dust. Assemble the table and legs, and finish the table by applying a coat of gloss varnish. For a really good finish you will need two or more coats, allowing each one to dry before applying the next.

Children's Nursery
Gallery

Teddy bear stool
This stool by Walnut Hollow, with its heart-shaped seat, has been painted with a stippled teddy bear design and would make an ideal gift.

Rocker
A charming miniature rocking horse painted in a stylized floral design by Priscilla Hauser, using FolkArt acrylic paints.

Miniature chair
This rustic dolls' chair was a junk shop find that has been sanded and repainted in simple brushstrokes to create a lovely item for a child's room.

Cradle
Lace, simply painted with dots and lines, can be amazingly effective. Here the lace has been painted in white over a country blue on to a doll's cradle.

Pansy Placemat and Coaster

Beth Blinston

P ansies are charming, small, cool-weather flowers. They come in many colours, with a variety of markings and flower sizes. These colourful pansies will brighten your table year round and painted on to a black background, they have a simple elegance.

1 Mix together deep midnight blue and lamp black paint in a ratio of 3:1. Using the flat brush, apply two base coats of this mix to both the placemat and the coasters. Trace the pansy design on page 94 and transfer the pattern on to the placemat by placing the transfer paper under the tracing and going over the design with a stylus or sharp pencil.

You will need

deep midnight blue
Hauser dark green
Hauser medium green
black green
Hauser light green
plantation pine
light buttermilk
dioxazine purple
ultra blue deep
cadmium yellow
marigold
violet haze
rookwood red
French vanilla
black plum
pansy lavender
cranberry wine
soft black
lamp black (not shown above)

Oval placemat and coaster
Acrylic paints, such as DecoArt Americana, as shown above
2.5 cm (1 in) flat brush
Tracing paper
White transfer paper
Stylus or sharp pencil
1 cm (⅜ in) angled shading brush
Small filbert brush
10/0 short liner brush
Clear varnish

2 Using the 1 cm (⅜ in) angled shading brush, paint the leaves marked D with Hauser dark green and the remaining leaves with Hauser medium green. Using the same brush, shade the medium green leaves with Hauser dark green where they meet the petals or other leaves. Shade the dark green leaves with black green.

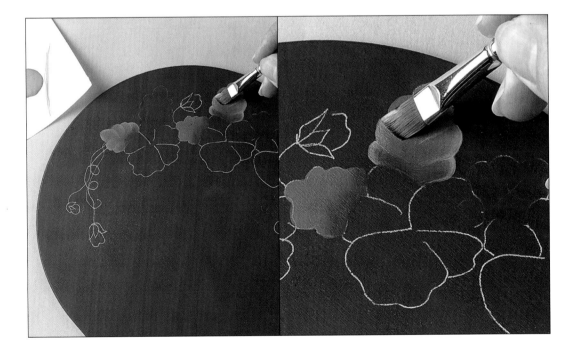

3 Highlight the medium green leaves with Hauser light green using an elongated "C" stroke to show the contours. Highlight the dark leaves with Hauser medium green.

4 Using the filbert brush loaded with a wash of plantation pine, paint one shape following stroke between the veins on all leaves. Reinforce the shading if necessary. To paint the veins, load the liner brush with Hauser light green and side-load with Hauser dark green.

5 To paint Pansy 2 (see template), load the 1 cm (⅜ in) angled shading brush with light buttermilk and paint in the four back petals. Pansies have five petals and are painted in sequence starting with the back petals. Paint petal 1 and slightly overlap this when painting petal 2. When painting petals 3 and 4, slightly overlap the bottom edge of petals 1 and 2. Petal 5 overlaps the bottom edge of petals 3 and 4.

6 Load the same brush with a 50:50 mix of dioxazine purple and ultra blue deep. Place the heel of the brush in the centre of the flower where the petals meet and then wriggle the toe of the brush in an arc around the top edge. Lay your brush down at angle so that the bristles bend a little on your board. Move the brush in a gentle, rounded zig-zag motion to create a ruffled edge.

7 Using the same brush loaded with cadmium yellow, highlight the edges of petal 2 with a ruffle.

8 Paint petals 3 and 4. Load the brush with marigold on the toe (long tip) and dioxazine purple on the heel. Place the heel of the brush in the centre of the flower where the petals meet and wriggle the toe of the brush in an arc around the outer edge. Lay your brush at an angle so the bristles bend a little on your board. Move the brush in a rounded zig-zag motion to create a ruffled edge.

9 Paint the whole of petal 5 in a coat of dioxazine purple. Allow to dry and then ruffle the edge with violet haze.

10 Using the liner brush, paint a cadmium yellow smile on to petal 5, just below the point where all the petals meet. Pull some fine stokes down on to petal 5. Add a few fine marigold strokes. Paint a spot of Hauser dark green above the smile and add a line of Hauser light green, rookwood red and then light buttermilk. Paint a small comma stroke either side of the spot you have just painted and take the tail of the commas down around the top edge of petal 5. Add some fine line turnbacks on any petals that you think may need a little more definition. Leave for 24 hours before spraying with two coats of clear varnish.

Colourways for remaining pansies

When you have finished painting all the pansies, leave for 24 hours before varnishing.

Pansy 1

Base with French vanilla and then ruffle in rookwood red on all the petals, leaving the centre of petal 2 showing. Wash petal 1 with black plum and a float of black plum to shade behind petals 5, 4, 3 and 2 where they overlap. Paint the beard on petals 3, 4 and 5 using the short liner brush loaded with black plum. Paint the buds using rookwood and black plum.

Buds 1, 2 and 3

Paint with rookwood red and black plum.

Pansy 2

See step-by-step instructions.

Bud 4

Paint with marigold on the toe of the brush and dioxazine purple on the heel.

Pansy 3

Block in all the petals with royal purple and highlight the edge with pansy lavender. Float black plum shade behind petals 5, 4, 3 and 2 where they overlap. Paint the beard on petals 3, 4 and 5 using the short liner brush loaded with black plum.

Pansy 4

Block in all the petals with light buttermilk. Ruffle in the edge of all the petals with cranberry wine.

Float a shade of black plum behind petals 5, 4, 3 and 2 where they overlap. Dry-brush all petals from the centre with soft black. Paint the beard on petals 3, 4 and 5 using the short liner brush loaded with black plum.

Bud 5

Paint with cranberry wine and dry-brush with soft black.

Pansy 5

Block in all the petals with a mix of dioxazine purple and ultra blue deep. Highlight the edges with a ruffle of violet haze.

Bud 6

Paint with violet haze on the toe of the brush and dioxazine purple on the heel.

Decorated Wall
and Table

Stephanie Weightman

reating a decorative paint effect on a wall can give a room a lovely, personal feel, especially when teamed with a matching dressing table. This type of painting is not hard to achieve and amateur painters will be able to create their own effects easily. Working freehand is fun and exciting – just be brave!

1 Make sure that the wall to be painted is smooth, clean, and dry. Position the table or other piece of furniture that you are "framing" and work out where you are going to position your design. Double-load a 2 cm (¾ in) brush with dark brown and wicker white and paint the vines using the chisel edge of the brush. Vary the thicknesses of the vines – it will look more realistic.

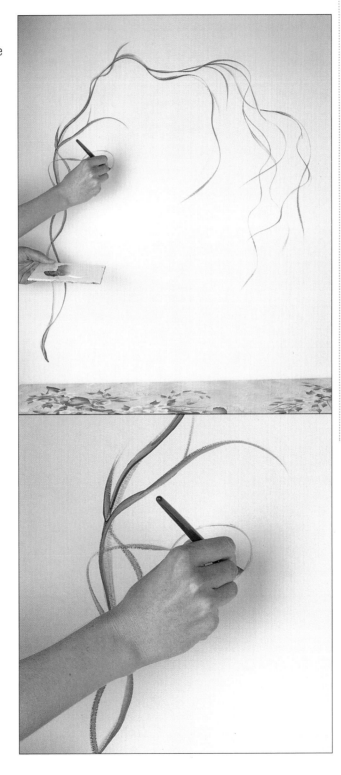

You will need

dark brown

wicker white

thicket

buttercream

settlers blue

periwinkle

butter pecan

school bus yellow

Wooden dressing table

Acrylic paints, such as FolkArt, as shown above

2 cm (¾ in) flat brush

Size 12 flat brush

Blending gel

Liner brush

2 Double-load a 2 cm (¾ in) flat brush in thicket and buttercream and paint the large leaves. Starting on the chisel edge and keeping the lighter colour to the inside of each leaf, "wiggle" the brush out to make one half of the leaf. Repeat for the other side to complete the leaf. Vary the direction of the leaves for interest.

3 Using the same brush, paint in the flower buds. Double-load with settlers blue and periwinkle and use "C" strokes. With the same colours and brush, paint in the larger petals throughout the design, using comma strokes. Vary the size of the roses and the direction they are facing in.

artist's tip

When painting the leaves, do not feel you have to completely rinse out your brush if you are changing to another green. A trace of the other colours adds harmony to your work.

4 Double-load the size 12 flat brush with thicket and buttercream. Add a few single-stroke filler leaves. Add more filler leaves, this time using thicket and butter pecan. Finally, add some shadow leaves using a mixture of butter pecan and blending gel. These leaves will be semi-transparent and should fill any gaps in the design.

5 Double-load the size 12 flat brush with butter pecan and wicker white and add some blossom, keeping the lighter colour to the centre of the flower. Each blossom has five "C" stroke petals, although you can vary the design. Paint the blossoms in small groups for a more realistic effect.

6 Add dots to the blossom centres using school bus yellow and the wooden tip of a liner brush handle. Finally, finish off the design by adding a few curly tendrils. Use a watered-down mix of thicket paint and the liner brush.

variation

To decorate a piece of furniture to match, simply make sure the surface to be painted is clean and dry. Paint on the elements in the same order as above.

Crackle and Gold Leaf Waste-bin

Try using crackle medium and gold leaf to smarten up an everyday object. This simple waste-bin has a classic feel and will make an elegant addition to any room. Gold leaf can be used on any number of objects – experiment by covering shells and stones or other found items. Crackle medium is simple and fun to use – just watch the crackles appear!

You will need

metallic glorious gold

buttermilk

MDF waste bin, approximately 23 cm (9 in) tall

Sanding pad

Soft cloths

Acrylic paints, such as DecoArt Americana, as shown above

Large flat brush

Pencil

Gold outliner

Crackling medium

Detail brush

Size (adhesive) for leaf metal

Imitation gold leaf sheets

Soft brush

1 Sand away any rough edges on the waste-bin and wipe over the surface with a clean cloth.

2 Paint the waste bin inside and outside with a coat of metallic glorious gold paint, using a large flat brush. Allow to dry.

3 Mark a line around the waste bin with a pencil, 4 cm (1½ in) from the top. Using the gold outliner, make a line of scrolls all around the bin, on this line. Allow to dry.

4 Using the large flat brush, paint the entire bin below the scroll line with an even coat of crackling medium. Leave to dry for about an hour.

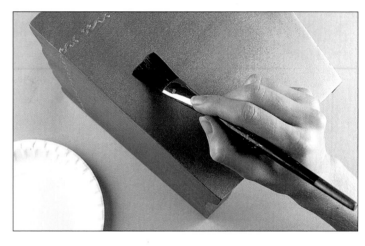

variation

Decorate an old pine or patterned mirror frame with imitation gold leaf sheets. Silver or copper sheets also work well.

5 Apply a contrasting coat of buttermilk acrylic paint over the crackling medium with the large flat brush, working quickly with downward strokes. The crackling will start within moments so only work on one section at a time and apply paint thickly so that it does not look streaky. Do not try to paint over the area again or the crackle effect will be spoiled.

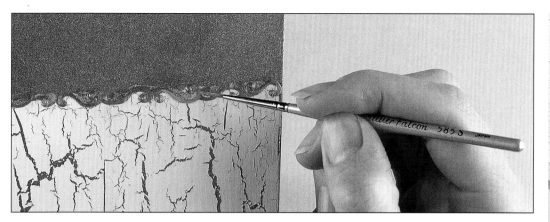

artist's tip
Don't throw away the excess flakes of gold leaf as they can be used for other, smaller projects.

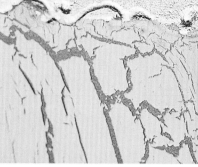

6 Using the detail brush, paint the scrolls with size for leaf metal, then, using a larger flat brush, paint the gold area above the scrolls with the size. Leave for about 15 minutes.

7 Lay the imitation gold sheets over the sized area, overlapping as necessary. Press the leaves gently with a soft clean cloth. Check the area is fully covered with leaf metal and leave for three hours.

8 Using a clean, dry, soft brush, work over the gold-leafed areas with soft circular movements to remove any excess metal leaf. You should have a smooth gilded surface.

variation
This technique can be used on all sorts of everyday items. This simple clock will sit perfectly on a mantlepiece.

Fuchsia Screen

Cathryn Wood

This cascading screen is ideal for hiding items from view and is great as a room divider. It is also an attractive item in its own right and is a great way of adding temporary, portable colour to a room. A perfect project if you are hesitant about painting on a wall.

You will need

wicker white

butter pecan

basil green

green forest

berry wine

Inca gold

licorice

Sandpaper

4 cm (1½ in) household paintbrush

Acrylic paints, such as FolkArt, as shown above

Glazing medium

2 cm (¾ in) flat brush

Plastic food wrap

Size 12 flat brush

Gold reflecting medium

Liner brush

Acrylic spray sealer

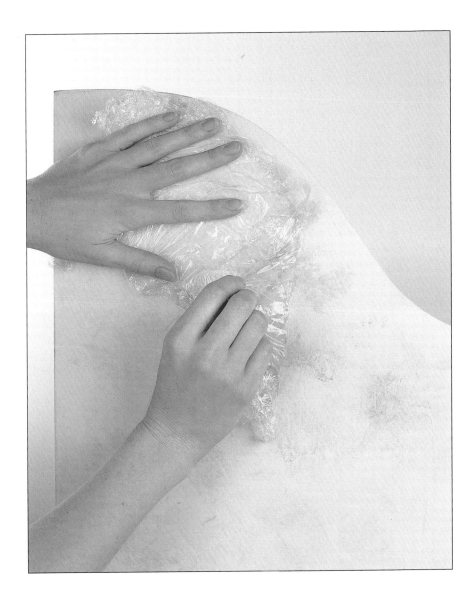

1 Prepare the screen to be painted, sanding if necessary. Apply a base coat in wicker white acrylic paint using a household paintbrush. Allow to dry. Make a scumble glaze with glazing medium and butter pecan acrylic paint using a ratio of six parts glaze to four parts paint. Roughly brush this on to the screen with the 2 cm (¾ in) brush, so that the background colour shows through. Take a sheet of plastic food wrap and place it over the wet glaze, moving it about with the palms of your hands. Peel back the cling film and continue until you have covered the whole area and created an attractive textured effect.

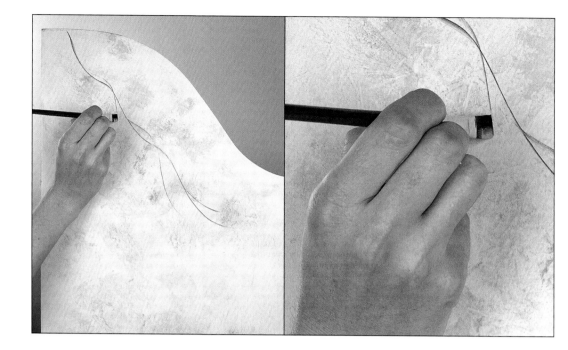

2 Double-load the size 12 flat brush with basil green and green forest and, working on the chisel edge of the brush, paint the vines. Criss-cross the vines for a more natural look.

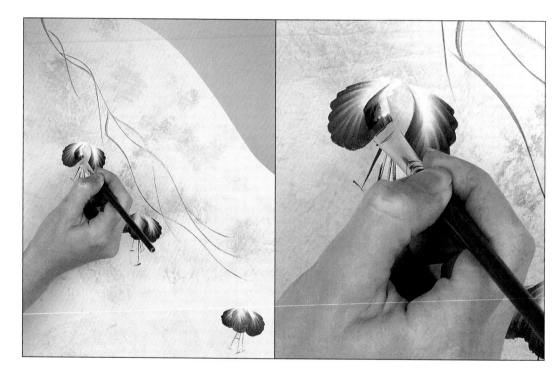

3 Double-load a size 12 brush with berry wine and wicker white. Working with the white to the inside, "wiggle" the brush to create the side petals of the fuchsia flower. Aim for a crinoline shape. Add three stamens with the chisel edge of the brush and then paint in the third, central petal.

4 Paint the seedpod at the top of the flower in the same colours by placing the brush on the chisel edge, with the white nearest the flower. Pivot the white and turn the berry wine to create a droplet shape. Add three pointed one-stroke petals, keeping the white uppermost. Add smaller one-stroke buds in the same colours.

5 Using the chisel edge of a size 12 brush, double-loaded with basil green and green forest, draw in the stalks. Add a calyx to each flower with a pivot stroke. Continue with large "wiggle" leaves and a few one-stroke leaves in the same colours. Paint smaller, one-stroke leaves in Inca gold in the spaces between the leaves. Add a few more leaves in gold reflecting medium to create shadow leaves that recede into the background.

6 To paint the hummingbird, double-load a size 12 brush with forest green and wicker white and paint the upper part of the head with a pivot stroke, with the green to the outside. Continue with the upper body, which is shaped like a long one-stroke leaf.

7 Double-load the same brush with berry wine and wicker white. Paint the lower body and head in the same way, keeping the white to the inside.

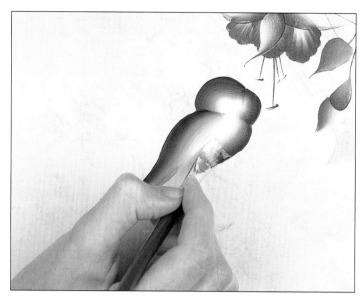

8 Add the back wing with a double-load of forest green and wicker white in the shape of a one-stroke leaf, keeping the green uppermost. Then add the front wing in the same way. Using the chisel edge of the same brush, and small extended comma strokes, add the wing and tail feathers, in the same colours, leading with the white.

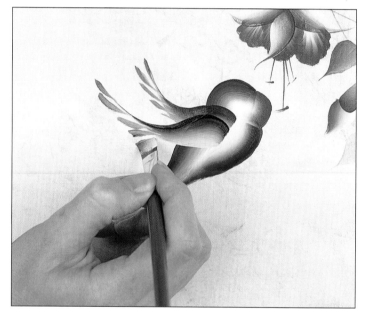

9 Paint in the eye using the liner brush and licorice. Paint a few fine lines above and below the eye and allow to dry. Add a white highlight to the eye using the liner brush. Add a few tendrils to the foliage using the liner brush and forest green, watered down to an inky consistency. Allow to dry before spraying with acrylic spray sealer.

Templates

To use any of the templates as they were used in the projects, you will need to enlarge the designs by the percentages given. The simplest way is to use a photocopier. If you wish to paint any of the designs on your own items you will need to photocopy to the size required.

Rosebud Platter
(page 32)
photocopy to 103%

Daisy Chair
(page 22)
photocopy to 110%

Berries and Blossom Mirror
(page 18)
photocopy to 100%

Ivy Kitchen Shelf
(page 26)
*photocopy to
117%*

Key Holder
(page 36)
photocopy to 110%

Rose Lamp

(page 46)

photocopy to 165%

*To fit a tray of any size
extend lines outwards
from the points arrowed*

Honeysuckle and

Blossom Tray

(page 54)

D

(3)

D

3

4

2

(4)

D

(5)

(6)

Pansy Placemat
and Coaster

(page 70)

*photocopy to
109%*

5

1

(2)

(1)

Tulip Watering Can

(page 40)

*photocopy to
116%*

Country Chest (page 58)
*For a draw width of 17cm photocopy at 200% then
photocopy the resulting photocopy again by 200%*

94

Suppliers and Useful Addresses

UK

The Biskit Tin
6 Regent Buildings
York Road, Acomb
York, YO26 4LT
Tel: 01904 787799
www.thebiskittin.co.uk
Craft and painting supplies

The British Association of Decorative and Folk Arts
c/o 153 High Street
Irthlingborough
Northants NN9 5PU
Tel: 07889 496001
www.badfa.net
Decorative painting association

DecoArt
STEP Business Centre
Wortley Road, Deepcar
Sheffield S36 2UH
Tel: 0114 290 3619
www.carolsykes.co.uk
DecoArt products and courses

Harvey Baker Design Ltd
Unit 1, Rodgers Ind. Estate
Yalberton Road, Paignton
Devon TQ4 7QG
Tel/Fax: 01803 521515
www.harvey-baker-design.co.uk
Suppliers of MDF blanks and galvanised ware

Hobbycraft
Unit 3 Westway Cross
Shopping Centre
Greenford
Middlesex UB6 0UW
Tel: 020 8747 7500
Craft and painting supplies

Ikea
Tel: 020 8208 5600
www.ikea.com
Call the above number for store information

National Creative Workshops
The Manor House
St. Lawrence Road
Northwingfield
Derbyshire, S42 7HX
Tel: 01773 511288
Fax: 01773 511911
www.ukonestroke.com
Mail order One-stroke painting supplies and courses

Northern Brushstrokes Teachers Society
Tel: 01909 591808
www.brushstrokesteachers.co.uk
Information on classes throughout the north of England

Scumble Goosie
Lewiston Mill
Toadsmoor Road,
Brimscombe, Stroud
Gloucestershire GL5 2TB
Tel: 01453 731305
www.scumble-goosie.co.uk
Suppliers of ready-to-paint furniture and accessories

The Stencil House
Vernon Road, Basford
Nottingham NG6 0BX
Tel: 0115 900 3531
www.stencilhouse.co.uk
Wholesale and mail order DecoArt products, decorative stencils, MDF blanks, Loew Cornell and FM brushes

Vale Woodcraft
Tel: 01623 810 110
www.valewoodcraft.co.uk
Suppliers of MDF blanks for painting

USA

DecoArt Inc
Highway 150 & 27
Stanford, KY 40484
Tel: 606 365 3193
www.decoart.com
Products for decorative painting

Plaid Enterprises Inc
3225 Westech Drive
Norcross, GA 30092 3500
Tel: 678 291 8100
www.plaidonline.com
Painting books, supplies and kits

The Society of Decorative Painters
393 North McLean Boulevard
Wichita, KS 67203-5968
Tel: 316 269 9300
www.decorativepainters.org
Decorative painting association

Walnut Hollow
1409 State Road 23
Dodgeville, WI 534533
Tel: 1 800 950 5101
www.walnuthollow.com
Suppliers of unfinished wood products and accessories

SOUTH AFRICA

Artes
3 Aylesbury Street
Bellville, 7530
Cape Town
Tel: 021 957 4525

Renaissance Art Shop
Shop 4, Ryneveld Plaza
Ryneveld Street
Stellenbosch, 7600
Cape Town
Tel: 021 886 5527

Art, Crafts and Hobbies
72 Hibernia Street
George, 6529
Tel: 044 874 1337
Retail and mail order

Bowker Arts and Crafts
52 4th Avenue
Newton Park, 6405
Port Elizabeth
Tel: 041 365 2487

Art Shop
140ᵃ Victoria Avenue
Benoni West, 1503
Johannesburg
Tel: 011 421 1030

Art, Stock and Barrel
Shop 44, Parklane Centre
12 Commercial Road
Pietermaritzburg, 3201
Tel: 033 342 1026

Shave Paint Centres
39 Old Main Road
Pinetown, 3610
Durban
Tel: 031 702 6315

Dulux Paint 'n Paper
75 Voortrekker Street
Bloemfontein, 9301
Tel: 051 430 3699

AUSTRALIA

Arts and Craft Centre
34 Mint Street
East Victoria Park
WA 6101
Tel: (08) 9361 4567

Websites:
www.dulux.com.au
www.wattyl.com.au
www.whiteknightpaints.com.au

NEW ZEALAND

Auckland Decorative Arts
591 Remuera Road
Upland Village
Auckland
Tel: 09 524 0936
Craft and decorative painting supplies

Studio Art Supplies
225 Parnell Road
Parnell, Auckland
Tel: 09 377 0302
Craft and decorative painting supplies

Resene Colour Shops and Resellers
www.resene.co.nz
Paint supplies

Spotlight Stores
Whangarei (09) 430 7220
Wairau Park (09) 444 0220
Henderson (09) 836 0888
Pamure (09) 527 0915
Manukau (09) 263 6760
Hamilton (07) 839 1793
Rotorua (07) 343 6901
New Plymouth (06) 757 3575
Hastings (06) 878 5223
Palmerston North (06) 357 6833
Porirua (04) 237 0650
Wellington (04) 472 5600
Christchurch (03) 377 6121
Dunedin (03) 477 1478
www.spotlight.net.nz
Wide range of craft and painting supplies

Visions and Dreams Ltd
Tel: 0800 427 238
Craft paints and stencils

Index

acetate sheet 47, 48
adhesive, to apply 13, 52, 63
antique effect 29
Antique "Leather" Writing Desk 50–3

base coat, to apply 14
Berries and Blossom Mirror 18–21
    template 91
Blinston, Beth: project by 70–5
brown paper, to smooth using 14, 65, 67
brush: care of 11
    flat, to use 10, 14, 15
    liner, to use 10–11, 16
    to load 14; see also double-loading
    round, to use 10, 15
    sponge 11
    types of 10–11

"C" stroke 15
Chair, Daisy 22–5
Chest, Country 58–63
Children's Nursery Gallery 68
clingfilm, to texture using 85
clock, crackle and gold leaf 83
Coaster, Pansy Placemat and 70–5
cocktail stick 13
colours, to blend 14
comma stroke 15, 16
cotton buds 13
Country Chest 58–63
    template 94
Crackle and Gold Leaf Waste-bin 80–3
crackle medium 81
    to apply 82

Daisy Chair 22–5
    template 91
Decorated Wall and Table 76–9
design sources 17
distressing 27, 33
dotting 13, 17, 62, 63
double-loading 14, 15

equipment 12–13
extender, to use 65, 67

faux marbling 65–7
Fruit Gallery 30
Fuchsia Screen 84–9

Garden Items Gallery 44
gilding cream, to apply 29
glass, to prepare 14
gold leaf 81
    to apply 83
gold outliner 82

hairbrush back 21
Haley, Paula: project by 36–9
Honeysuckle and Blossom Tray 54–7
    template 93
Horsfield, Cynthia: project by 54–7

Italian Marble Table 64–7
Ivy Kitchen Shelf 26–9
    template 92

Key Holder 36–9
    template 92
Kitchen Shelf, Ivy 26–9

Lamp, Rose 46-9
lampshade 49
leather effect 52–3
leaves, to create 15
limewashed effect 27

marbling, faux 65–7
masking 13, 55
MDF, to prepare 13, 14, 51, 55, 67, 81
metal, to prepare 14, 41
Mirror, Berries and Blossom 18–21
mirror frame 18–21, 82
Myers, Ann: project by 40–3

one-stroke technique 33–5

paint, acrylic 12
paint mediums 12
painting groups 17
palette 12
palette knife 13
Pansy Placemat and Coaster 70–5
    template 94
pen holder 53, 63
petals, to create 15
Placemat and Coaster, Pansy 70–5
plant pot 43
plastic, to prepare 23
Platter, Rosebud 32–5
preparation see surface preparation

Rose Lamp 46–9
    template 93
Rosebud Platter 32–5
template 90
ruffle 16

"S" stroke 15
sanding 13, 14, 51, 59, 67, 81
    see also surface preparation
sandpaper 13, 14
    see also sanding

Screen, Fuchsia 84–9
scumble glaze 85
sealing 12, 19
Shelf, Ivy Kitchen 26–9
sponge 13
sponging 17, 55
stems, to create 16
stippling 17
stylus, to use 17, 62, 63
surface preparation 13, 14
    glass 14
    MDF 13, 14, 51, 55, 67, 81
    metal 14, 41
    plastic 23
    plywood 59
Sykes, Carol: project by 32–5

Table, Decorated Wall and 76–9
Table, Italian Marble 64–7
tipping 15
tissue paper, to create "leather" look with 52–3
tracing 13, 17
transfer paper 17, 19
Tray, Honeysuckle and Blossom 54–7
Tulip Watering Can 40–3
    template 94

varnish 12, 67

Wall and Table, Decorated 76–9
Waste-bin, Crackle and Gold Leaf 80–3
Watering Can, Tulip 40-3
Weightman, Stephanie: projects by 46–9, 64–7, 76–9
Wood, Cathryn: project by 84–9
Writing Desk, Antique "Leather" 50–3